Series Editor: Pie Corbett

CAMBRIDGE UNIVERSITY PRESS
Cambridge, New York, Melbourne, Madrid, Cape Town, Singapore,
São Paulo, Delhi

Cambridge University Press
The Edinburgh Building, Cambridge CB2 8RU, UK

www.cambridge.org
Information on this title: www.cambridge.org/9780521618939

First published 2006
Reprinted 2008

Printed in Dubai by Oriental Press

A catalogue record for this publication is available from the British Library

ISBN 978-0-521-61893-9 paperback

ACKNOWLEDGEMENTS
Cover: Nick Diggory

Artwork: Beehive Illustration (Russell Becker, Omar, Peter Richardson);
Illustration (Nick Diggory, Bill Greenhead, Matthew Robson)

Layout and page design by HL Studios

Texts: "Night Mail" by W. H. Auden; "I Am the Song" and "Timothy Winters" by
Charles Causley from *Collected Poems for Children* published by Macmillan; "City
Jungle" and "Spanish Holiday Haiku" by Pie Corbett; "The Oldest Girl in the
World" by Carol Ann Duffy; "The Cat's Muse" by Philip Gross; "Amulet",
"Leaves", "Autumn Song" and "The Warm and the Cold" by Ted Hughes,
published by Faber and Faber; "The Listeners" by Walter de la Mare as printed
in *The Complete Poems of Walter de la Mare* 1969 (USA: 1970); "Give and Take"
and "Joy at the Sound" by Roger McGough from *Good Enough to Eat* (© Roger
McGough 2000) are reproduced by permission of PFD (www.pfd.co.uk) on
behalf of Roger McGough; "Not Only" and "The River's Story" (© Brian Patten
2000 / 1990 / 1985) reproduced by permission of the author c/o Rogers,
Coleridge & White Ltd, 20 Powis Mews, London W11 1JN; "Grannie" by Vernon
Scannell; "Spring" and "Summer" from *The British Museum – Haiku* translated
by R. H. Blyth (© R. H. Blyth. Permission given by Hokuseido Press); "Summer"
translated by D. J. Cobb, previously published in *Haiku* (British Museum Press,
2002), reproduced by permission of D. J. Cobb.

Contents

Established
poets

The Listeners

"Is there anybody there?" said the Traveller,

Knocking on the moonlit door;

And his horse in the silence champed the grasses

Of the forest's ferny floor:

And a bird flew up out of the turret,

Above the Traveller's head:

And he smote upon the door again a second time;

"Is there anybody there?" he said.

But no one descended to the Traveller;

No head from the leaf-fringed sill

Leaned over and looked into his grey eyes,

Where he stood perplexed and still.

But only a host of phantom listeners

That dwelt in the lone house then

Stood listening in the quiet of the moonlight

To that voice from the world of men:

Stood thronging the faint moonbeams on the

    dark stair,

That goes down to the empty hall,

Hearkening in an air stirred and shaken

By the lonely Traveller's call.

And he felt in his heart their strangeness,

Their stillness answering his cry,

While his horse moved, cropping the dark turf,

'Neath the starred and leafy sky;

For he suddenly smote on the door, even

Louder, and lifted his head:

"Tell them I came, and no one answered,

That I kept my word," he said.

Never the least stir made the listeners,

Though every word he spake

Fell echoing through the shadowiness of the still house

From the one man left awake:

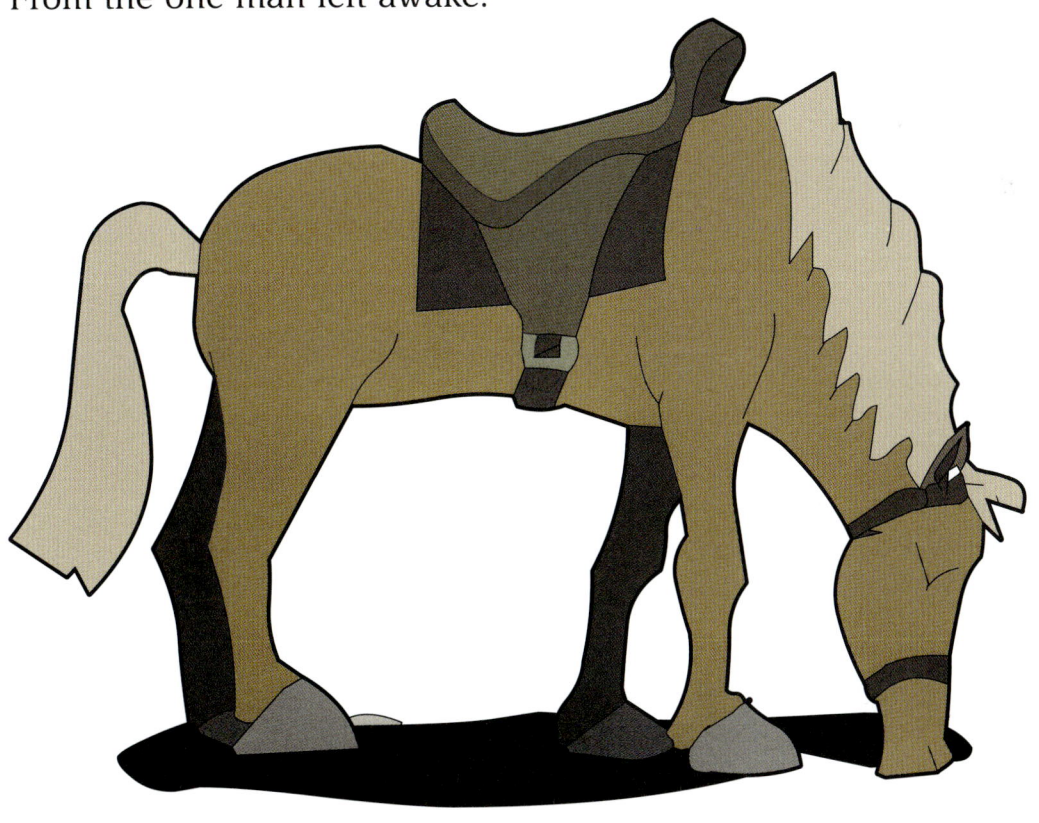

Ay, they heard his foot upon the stirrup,

And the sound of iron on stone,

And how the silence surged softly backward,

When the plunging hoofs were gone.

Walter de la Mare

Amulet

Inside the wolf's fang, the mountain of heather.

Inside the mountain of heather, the wolf's fur.

Inside the wolf's fur, the ragged forest.

Inside the ragged forest, the wolf's foot.

Inside the wolf's foot, the stony horizon.

Inside the stony horizon, the wolf's tongue.

Inside the wolf's tongue, the doe's tears.

Inside the doe's tears, the frozen swamp.

Inside the frozen swamp, the wolf's blood.

Inside the wolf's blood, the snow wind.

Inside the snow wind, the wolf's eye.

Inside the wolf's eye, the North star.

Inside the North star, the wolf's fang.

Ted Hughes

I Am the Song

I am the song that sings the bird.

I am the leaf that grows the land.

I am the tide that moves the moon.

I am the stream that halts the sand.

I am the cloud that drives the storm.

I am the earth that lights the sun.

I am the fire that strikes the stone.

I am the clay that shapes the hand.

I am the word that speaks the man.

Charles Causley

Night Mail

This is the night mail crossing the border,

Bringing the cheque and the postal order,

Letters for the rich, letters for the poor,

The shop at the corner and the girl next door.

Pulling up Beattock, a steady climb –

The gradient's against her, but she's on time.

Past cotton grass and moorland boulder

Shovelling white steam over her shoulder,

Snorting noisily as she passes

Silent miles of wind-bent grasses.

Birds turn their heads as she approaches,

Stare from the bushes at her blank-faced coaches.

Sheep-dogs cannot turn her course,

They slumber on with paws across.

In the farm she passes no one wakes,

But a jug in the bedroom gently shakes.

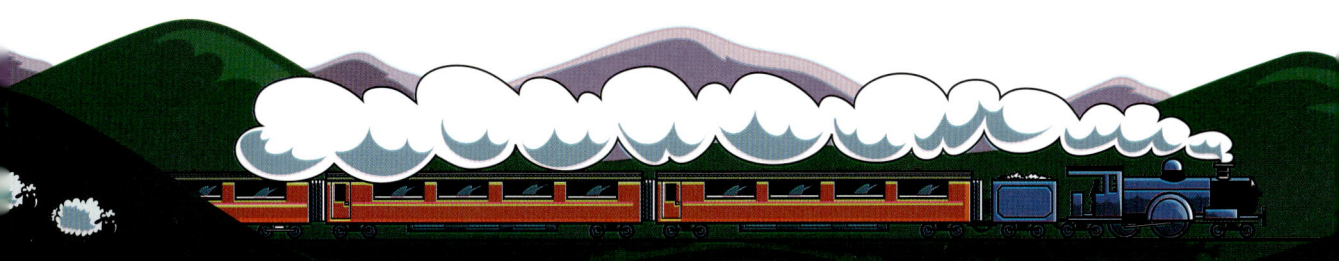

Dawn freshens, the climb is done.

Down towards Glasgow she descends

Towards the steam tugs yelping down the glade of cranes,

Towards the fields of apparatus, the furnaces

Set on the dark plain like gigantic chessmen.

All Scotland waits for her:

In the dark glens beside the pale-green lochs

Men long for news.

Letters of thanks, letters from banks,

Letters of joy from girl and boy,

Receipted bills and invitations

To inspect new stock or visit relations,

And applications for situations,

And timid lovers' declarations,

And gossip, gossip from all the nations,

News circumstantial, news financial,

Letters with holiday snaps to enlarge in,

Letters with faces scrawled in the margin,

Letters from uncles, cousins, and aunts,

Letters to Scotland from the South of France,

Letters of condolence to Highlands and Lowlands,

Notes from overseas to Hebrides –

Written on paper of every hue;

The pink, the violet, the white and the blue,

The chatty, the catty, the boring, adoring,

The cold and official and the heart's outpouring,

Clever, stupid, short and long,

The typed and the printed and the spelt all wrong.

Thousands are still asleep

Dreaming of terrifying monsters

Or a friendly tea beside the band at Cranston's or Crawford's.

Asleep in working Glasgow, asleep in well-set Edinburgh,

Asleep in granite Aberdeen.

They continue their dreams;

But shall wake soon and long for letters.

And none will hear the postman's knock

Without a quickening of the heart,

For who can hear and feel

　　　himself forgotten?

W. H. Auden

Leaves

Who's killed the leaves?

Me, says the apple, I've killed them all.

Fat as a bomb or a cannonball

I've killed the leaves.

Who sees them drop?

Me, says the pear, they will leave me all bare

So all the people can point and stare.

I see them drop.

Who'll catch their blood?

Me, me, me, says the marrow, the marrow.

I'll get so rotund that they'll need a wheelbarrow.

I'll catch their blood.

Who'll make their shroud?

Me, says the swallow, there's just time enough

Before I must pack all my spools and be off.

I'll make their shroud.

Who'll dig their grave?

Me, says the river, with the power of the clouds

A brown deep grave I'll dig under my floods.

I'll dig their grave.

Who'll be their parson?

Me, says the Crow, for it is well-known

I study the bible right down to the bone.

I'll be their parson.

Who'll be their chief mourner?

Me, says the wind, I will cry through the grass

The people will pale and go cold when I pass.

I'll be chief mourner.

Who'll carry the coffin?

Me, says the sunset, the whole world will weep

To see me lower it into the deep.

I'll carry the coffin.

Who'll sing a psalm?

Me, says the tractor, with my gear grinding glottle

I'll plough up the stubble and sing through my throttle.

I'll sing the psalm.

Who'll toll the bell?

Me, says the robin, my song in October

Will tell the still gardens the leaves are over.

I'll toll the bell.

Ted Hughes

City Jungle

Rain splinters town.

Lizard cars cruise by;
their radiators grin.

Thin headlights stare –
shop doorways keep
their mouths shut.

At the roadside
hunched houses cough.

Newspapers shuffle by,
hands in their pockets.
The gutter gargles.

A motorbike snarls;
dustbins flinch.

Streetlights bare
their yellow teeth.
The motorway's cat-black tongue
lashes across
the glistening back
of the tarmac night.

Pie Corbett

Poetry revision

Grannie

I stayed with her when I was six then went

To live elsewhere when I was eight years old.

For ages I remembered her faint scent

Of lavender, the way she'd never scold

No matter what I'd done, and most of all

The way her smile seemed, somehow, to enfold

My whole world like a warm, protective shawl.

I knew that I was safe when she was near,

She was so tall, so wide, so large, she would

Stand mountainous between me and my fear,

Yet oh, so gentle, and she understood

Every hope and dream I ever had.

She praised me lavishly when I was good,

But never punished me when I was bad.

Years later war broke out and I became

A soldier and was wounded while in France.

Back home in hospital, still very lame,

I realized suddenly that circumstance

Had brought me close to that small town where she

Was living still. And so I seized the chance

To write and ask if she could visit me.

She came. And I still vividly recall

The shock that I received when she appeared

That dark cold day. Huge grannie was so small!

A tiny, frail, old lady. It was weird.

She hobbled through the ward to where I lay

And drew quite close and, hesitating, peered.

And then she smiled: and love lit up the day.

Vernon Scannell

Timothy Winters

Timothy Winters comes to school
With eyes as wide as a football pool,
Ears like bombs and teeth like splinters:
A blitz of a boy is Timothy Winters.

His belly is white, his neck is dark,
And his hair is an exclamation mark.
His clothes are enough to scare a crow
And through his britches the blue winds blow.

When teacher talks he won't hear a word
And he shoots down dead the arithmetic-bird,
He licks the patterns off his plate
And he's not even heard of the Welfare State.

Timothy Winters has bloody feet
And he lives in a house on Suez Street,
He sleeps in a sack on the kitchen floor
And they say there aren't boys like him any more.

Old Man Winters likes his beer

And his missus ran off with a bombardier,

Grandma sits in the grate with a gin

And Timothy's dosed with an aspirin.

The Welfare Worker lies awake

But the law's as tricky as a ten-foot snake,

So Timothy Winters drinks his cup

And slowly goes on growing up.

At Morning Prayers the Master helves

For children less fortunate than ourselves,

And the loudest response in the room is when

Timothy Winters roars "Amen!"

So come one angel, come on ten:

Timothy Winters says "Amen

Amen amen amen amen."

Timothy Winters, Lord.

Amen.

Charles Causley

The Cat's Muse

I'm a tabby flabby house cat, just a fusty ball of fur,

A never-caught-a-mouse cat with a rusty sort of purr.

But sit down on the hearth mat and watch the fire with me.

I'll show you some of the dark and wild cats up my family tree.

Oh I'm no common-or-garden cat.

There's something you might miss:

the sabre teeth that I unsheath

when I stretch and yawn like this.

Sheba was a temple cat in Tutankhamun's days.

She had a hundred priestesses and several hundred slaves.

She curled up on an altar on a bed of purple silk,

Off saucers made of beaten gold she dined on camel's milk.

Oh I'm no common-or-garden cat.

My pedigree tends to show.

My tail is like a cobra

when it lashes to and fro.

Captain Moggan was a ship's cat and

he sailed the Spanish Main.

He went all the way around Cape Horn and made it home again.

His claws were sharp as cutlasses. His life was sharp and short.

He died in Valparaiso, leaving kittens in every port.

Oh I'm no common-or-garden cat.

Haven't you noticed my

one lop ear like a pirate's hat

that flops across my eye?

Greymalkin was a black magic cat with fur as slick as pitch.

She held covens in a cavern with a wild and wicked witch.

And when she went out hunting on a moonlit winter's night

The village folk would bar their doors and dogs dropped dead
with fright.

Oh I'm no common-or-garden cat.

Who knows what I might do?

You'd better keep me happy

or I'll put a spell…

…on…

…YOU!

Philip Gross

The River's Story

I remember when life was good.

I shilly-shallied across the meadows,

Tumbled down mountains,

I laughed and gurgled through the woods,

Stretched and yawned in a myriad of floods.

Insects, weightless as sunbeams,

Settled upon my skin to drink.

I wore lily-pads like medals.

Fish, lazy and battle-scarred,

Gossiped beneath them.

The damselflies were my ballerinas,

The pike my ambassadors.

Kingfishers, disguised as rainbows,

Were my secret agents.

It was a sweet time, a gone-time,

A time before factories grew,

Brick by greedy brick,

And left me cowering

In monstrous shadows.

Like drunken giants

They vomited their poisons into me.

Tonight, a scattering of vagrant bluebells,

Dwarfed by those same poisons,

Toll my ending.

Children, come and find me if you wish.

I am your inheritance.

Behind the derelict housing estates

You will discover my remnants.

Clogged with garbage and junk

To an open sewer I've shrunk.

I, who have flowed through history,

Who have seen hamlets become villages,

Villages become towns, towns become cities,

Am reduced to a trickle of filth

Beneath the still, burning stars.

Brian Patten

Give and Take

I give you clean air

You give me poisonous gas.

I give you mountains

You give me quarries.

I give you pure snow

You give me acid rain.

I give you spring fountains

You give me toxic canals.

I give you a butterfly

You gave me a plastic bottle.

I give you a blackbird

You gave me a stealth bomber.

I give you abundance

You give me waste.

I give you one last chance

You give me excuse after excuse.

Roger McGough

Joy at the Sound

Joy at the silver birch in the morning sunshine

Joy at the spring-green of its fingertips

Joy at the swirl of cold milk in the blue bowl

Joy at the blink of its bubbles

Joy at the cat revving up on the lawn

Joy at the frogs that leapfrog to freedom

Joy at the screen that fizzes to life

Joy at The Simpsons, Lisa and Bart

Joy at the dentist: "Fine, see you next year"

Joy at the school gates: "Closed"

Joy at the silver withholding the chocolate

Joy at the poem, two verses to go

Joy at the zing of the strings of the racquet

Joy at the bounce of the bright yellow ball

Joy at the key unlocking the door

Joy at the sound of her voice in the hall

Roger McGough

Themed poems

The Oldest Girl in the World

Children, I remember how I could hear

with my soft young ears

the tiny sounds of the air –

tinkles and chimes

like minuscule bells

ringing continually there;

clinks and chinks

like glasses of sparky gooseberry wine,

jolly and glinting and raised in the air.

Yes, I could hear like a bat. And how!

Can't hear a sniff of it now.

Truly, believe me, I could all the time see

every insect that crawled in a bush,

every bird that hid in a tree,

individually.

If I wanted to catch a caterpillar

to keep as a pet in a box

I had only to watch a cabbage

and there it would be,

crawling bendy and green towards me.

Yes, I could see with the eyes of a cat. Miaow!

Can't see a sniff of it now.

And my sense of taste was second to none.

By God, the amount I knew with my tongue!

The shrewd taste of a walnut's brain.

The taste of a train from a bridge.

Of a kiss. Of air chewy with midge.

Of fudge from a factory two miles away

from the house where I lived.

I'd stick out my tongue

to savour the sky in a droplet of rain.

Yes, I could taste like the fang of a snake! Wow!

Can't taste a sniff of it now.

On the scent, what couldn't I smell

with my delicate nose, my nostrils of pearl?

I could smell the world!

Snow. Soot. Soil.

Satsumas in their Christmas sock.

The ink of a pen.

The stink of an elephant's skin.

The blue broth of a swimming pool. Dive in!

The showbizzy gasp of the wind.

Yes, I could smell like a copper's dog. Bow-wow!

Can't smell a sniff of it now.

Carol Ann Duffy

The Warm and the Cold

Freezing dusk is closing
   Like a slow trap of steel
On trees and roads and hills and all
   That can no longer feel.
      But the carp is in its depth
         Like a planet in its heaven.
      And the badger in its bedding
         Like a loaf in the oven.
      And the butterfly in its mummy
         Like a viol in its case.
      And the owl in its feathers
         Like a doll in its lace.

Freezing dusk has tightened
   Like a nut screwed tight
On the starry aeroplane
   Of the soaring night.
      But the trout is in its hole
         Like a chuckle in a sleeper.
      The hare strays down the highway
         Like a root going deeper.
      The snail is dry in the outhouse

Like a seed in a sunflower.

The owl is pale on the gatepost

Like a clock on its tower.

Moonlight freezes the shaggy world

Like a mammoth of ice

The past and the future

Are the jaws of a steel vice.

But the cod is in the tide-rip

Like a key in a purse.

The deer are on the bare-blown hill

Like smiles on a nurse.

The flies are behind the plaster

Like the lost score of a jig.

Sparrows are in the ivy-clump

Like money in a pig.

Such a frost

The flimsy moon

Hast lost her wits.

A star falls.

The sweating farmers

Turn in their sleep

Like oxen on spits.

Ted Hughes

Autumn Song

There came a day that caught the summer

Wrung its neck

Plucked it

And ate it.

Now what shall I do with the trees?

The day said, the day said.

Strip them bare, strip them bare.

Let's see what is really there.

And what shall I do with the sun?

The day said, the day said.

Roll him away till he's cold and small.

He'll come back rested if he comes back at all.

And what shall I do with the birds?

The day said, the day said.

The birds I've frightened, let them flit,

I'll hang out pork for the brave tomtit.

And what shall I do with the seed?

The day said, the day said.

Bury it deep, see what it's worth.

See if it can stand the earth.

What shall I do with the people?

The day said, the day said.

Stuff them with apple and blackberry pie –

They'll love me then till the day they die.

There came this day and he was autumn.

His mouth was wide

And red as a sunset.

His tail was an icicle.

Ted Hughes

Haiku

Spring and Summer

the dawn of day –
on the tip of the barley leaf
the frost of spring
Onitsura

treading on the tail
of the copper pheasant
the setting sun of spring
Buson

a clear waterfall –
into the ripples
fall green pine-needles
Bashō

fresh young leaves –
the sound of a waterfall
both far and near
Buson

Spanish Holiday Haiku

Flies stalk the cup's rim –
washing their hands, fidgeting
in the sullen heat.

The sun sweats, hills shake.
The landscape does nothing too.
The pool is ice cool.

Distant hill lies still

like a sleeping lion, crouching.

An eagle hovers.

Pencil dragonflies,

in slim, pastel blue hover,

shivering, pool-side.

Daisy's wasp sting –

like a white injection mark –

a soft swollen moon.

Trying to sleep but

the room is far too stuffy –

even pillows sweat.

Pie Corbett